NEBRASKA

NEBR

ASKA

POEMS

Kwame Dawes

UNIVERSITY OF NEBRASKA PRESS   LINCOLN

© 2019 by the Board of Regents of the University of Nebraska

Acknowledgments for the use of copyrighted material appear on page xi,

which constitutes an extension of the copyright page.

Library of Congress Control Number: 2019946566

Set and designed in Filosofia by N. Putens.

For

Lorna

Sena, Kekeli, and Akua

For

Gwyneth, Kojo, Adjoa, and Kojovi

For

Mama the Great

And remembering

Neville and Aba

Honestly, it's not for everyone. —NEBRASKA STATE SLOGAN, 2018

CONTENTS

II

III

ACKNOWLEDGMENTS

The New Yorker: "Before Winter"

Tangling with the Epic (Peepal Tree Press, 2019): [The air now changes], "On History," "Fledge"

Punta del Burro (Janus Press, 2018): "Dark Season"

A New Beginning, with John Kinsella (Peepal Tree Press, 2018): "Novela," "The Scent of the Cankerworm," "The Quality of Light," "The Chronicler of Sorrows," "Sancho Panza," "The Messiness of Place"

In the Name of Our Families, with John Kinsella (Peepal Tree Press, 2020): "The Enemy of Memory," "The Poor Man's Sacrifice," "Bones," "Sponge," "In These Times," "Sugar," "July Fourth," "Falling Away," "On Picking Battles," "The Exile Remembers His Sisters"

Plume: "Long Distance"

32 Poems: "On Blindness"

Bosque: "Stumbling"

Special thanks to Jamaica Baldwin for help in digging up these poems and to Jeremy Poynting for his generous and indispensable editorial eye. Thanks to Marianne Kunkel for assistance with selections and for being a generous friend of my poems. With much gratitude to Donna Shear and the remarkable University of Nebraska Press team of editors, designers, and marketers for treating this work with care and consummate professionalism. With gratitude to the Department of English at the University of Nebraska–Lincoln for giving me the space to do this work. Special thanks to Ashley Strosnider at *Prairie Schooner* for support and for being a splendid sounding board.

NEBRASKA

The air now changes with the light and soft winds
across the prairie—it is November
the season of leaves, the light sussussuing,
sensual as bright autumnal rain scattered
over the last greens. I will remember
the discretion of seasons, the kindness
of light, and the silence of these wide lanes.
I will miss these, I'm sure, but little else
will feed nostalgia. No great loss and no regrets.

How I Became an Apostle

After Edward Hirsch

Now that I have my thorn in the flesh,
I can write epistles, holy writs. It's winter.

I limp out just after the delicate chaos
of flurries covers the driveway and I shovel.

This is a ritual of sin: after clearing a long
path, behind me the pox of snow returns.

The angel, remember, stopped fighting when
I broke his hip, tore his ligaments, as we say.

Now mine throbs deep inside muscle, bone, and fat,
and in this cold the pain purifies me.

By dusk I can barely walk, my foot drags across
the frozen driveway as the snow falls heavily.

My first epistle to the saints is a prayer pleading
that this, too, will pass. The snow covers multitudes.

Advent

Christmas falls on a Friday—the long week
of labor and waiting is gray with dull light,
and gradually the gloom fills my bones—
I have declared myself a fat man once too often.
Here in Nebraska I have learned the art
of restraint—hoarding lamentations and complaints;
how to hold my tongue until it is clear
that those around me have unlearned
the rituals of compassion; they cannot see
the despair in my eyes. Remember when
we knew that simply speaking out, our bile
would release it from our bodies,
that leeching chemistry of confession or hoping?
Not here. Here the body creates a membrane
of such leathery resilience that it may
keep in all the wounds we have collected.
And here in the slow march to Christmas,
I grow bloated with decency; and I have
decided to grow my beard again—the uniform
of a man pioneering the wilderness. At church,
the choir did not sing a Christmas song—
it is as if someone forgot the season—
but the pastors and elders all wore suits
and ties; while we clapped our hands

to the radio songs—good, clean Jesus
of Chick-fil-A and Texas charm. Look
at my eyes. Pay attention. Clouds, slow moving,
across the prairie sky—so slow it is as if
nothing is moving across the bigness of things.

The Barking Geese of Edenton

At four o'clock the heavy swoop of night is coming,
we walk, man and dog though our pedigrees
suggest nothing of the archetypal companionship,
we would be strained companions in the wilderness,
company, yes, but death would mean only
the loss of habit. Though at the top of the street,
the geese begin this barking through the air—
it is winter, and there they are, as if
their migration was delayed—they fill the sky
with the sharp angles of triangular formation;
and in this instant, we stop, look upward
trying to follow the pattern of their flight—
this, we share. Upstairs in my home, our
guest, the celebrated novelist, weeps at night,
between his genius is the darkness of loss;
he has lost a lover, she will not answer him,
and he is making bargains with God;
he grows thin, can't sleep. We meet in the plush
light of our dining room and talk
of the barking geese, the snow on the ground,
and the calculations of fame. This is the tail
end of a year. All the world is waiting
for some calamity; some bomb to explode.
Sure, we will die, each of us, this is
the truth. I study our faces like one studies the dead.

The Immigrant Contemplates Death

The man who carries his yoga
mat rolled up under his arm
walking through his city is the man
I have longed to be. It is as
if he will live forever. This
is what I can say of exile;
a body like me has lost track
of the narrative of mortality.
It is the brittle dry air
of these prairies, the wide-open
fields, the soil that has
grown too hard for burial,
it is easy to mistake
the longevity of farm people,
of white Lutheran stock,
for kindred souls. I was born
in a city that turned into
a village within hearing
distance, and the deep red
soil of Accra knows it is
always prepared for the deep
warmth of cankering bodies,
for the spirits that treat
the trees and roads as temporary
dwellings before the teeming
underneath of performance. In Kingston,

I considered death each day,
its friendship with the living;
and we die as if the body
was made for this. It is true
that among these midwestern
people I can forget myself—
I can forget that the deep
funk in my skin is my
brokenness steaming in
these late days of my life. Even
my doctor thinks I will live
longer; but I know that
the back end of this year, when
Lincoln's earth grows stony
with hoarfrost, I will land
in St. Mary, walk out into
the morning barefooted, un-shirted
and stand in the soft dark
soil, my weight pressing me
into its familiar give and embrace.
And this warm circling of air
is the comfort of all saints
to gain, and gain and gain.

Fledge

On long walks across the calming whiteness
of deep winter—the arctic air has walked in
and settled over everything—I dress
in dark colors, and venture out, breathing
what feels like a cleansing but is the grim
ritual of a man, constantly on edge
as if waiting for tomorrow's ill winds
to shatter the brittle calm. But to fledge
is all I want; to take flight off this icy edge.

Longing for the Hall of the Deaf

At the end of it there is this thing—words;
we collect them as people moving through
crowds collect germs; their bodies speaking
to each other, the scent, the leaping insects,
the flow of blood—an old woman reminds
you that the menstrual regimes of women
whisper their monthly rendezvous—
"the scientists have not done this, but I have—
and I have calculated that twelve feet
or the distance for eyes to make contact,
or for the sweat emanating from a woman's
thighs, for this to happen. And women,
who live countries away, if they talk
each day, somehow the cadence of their voices
finds a strange chemical echo,
and this too is magic, but is science;
and these are the miracles we know—
what of those we don't." It was her
way of saying her death is not cause
for mourning, though she said
she would hate for the ritual of black,
the commitment to memory in the act
of black for a year to be ignored. Death
is ordinary except when it is caused
by the calculations of vengeance
and willful neglect. Then it is extraordinary.

These lines across the page are not
songs—such music belongs to the magician.
No, these are mere conjuring,
they are spells, in the way that
remembering can be an incantation
for light. Outside the temperature
has dropped to minus two,
and everything is static in the air,
such a dry prairie cruelty, the cold
that has killed and will kill again.
What we make of the silences
of the epoch is what we make
of art. This is my dream: that my
words may be a grand infection
turning and turning in a bare
studio, our bodies electrified
to passions each time we walk
across a ribbon of imagination;
a kind of holy beauty consuming body.

The Midwestern Sky

Not all skies are readable. I am an alien
in this wide-open country, and the sky's
inscrutable dialect leaves me bewildered,
lost in what we must call a pastiche
of cliché. I can see in the squint
of old farmers moving along the market
lanes, husband holding the hand of wife,
both unsteadily stepping with the determination
of people who were trained to kneel
and pray each night—the ritual
is the truth—in their faces one knows
that the wisdom is there—the knowledge
of the sky's language—they have
read it with only a hint of spirit—
certain that it is not the sky
that is the mystery, but those who worship
it. These Lutherans will never worship
the sky—but treat its constancy
with the acceptance of faith, devotion,
duty. In time, I fear, I, too,
will turn this questioning into silence,
and I will welcome death as one
welcomes the winds from the west,
deep in winter—with resignation,
and with nothing of the pulsing
delight that fear can fill our hearts with.

First Winter

In Nebraska the promise
of blizzards, the gruff
edge of prairie storms
the kind the frozen
farmers and German
pioneers huddled against
in barns, praying
for the mercy of Indian
arrowheads, the cold
of the miserable,
the thing that explains
what is called stoic
Lutheran resolve;
the language of sordid
gratitude for the gasp
of spring, they
promised me all this
would make me
strong, better, a man—
the winter stayed
away, left me
to be fat, and southern
as I always have been,
nursing gout.

Loneliness

I have taken to talking to trees
in midwinter; never those at the edges
the safe ones gazing at the highway;

I go deep inside where the snow
is powdery, crystal under light.

We talk, the branches rub together
like insects hissing

the cold calms even my jittery heart;
the silence is absolute here.

Each step I am startled by the hollow
echo of leather on brittle snow.

Dark Season

It is the dark time, my dear,
so hard now to wake, my body

is battered with aches, as if
this stone sensible bed has

vowed to punish my sins. It is
the dark season, the air wet

with mist, and the sun, reluctant
to come before the rituals

of the day are almost over, this
is the season of intrigue

and betrayal, and not far
from the center of the world

the incumbent loses
his ability to count his votes

his stutter grows into a full
affectation in his panic. I know

this, and a greasy challenger,
high forehead and plastic

hair is soaring—these are
dark times, my love,

and I am trying for calm,
but the fears come in the silent

time, the knocks and groans
of a house still seething

into the ground, startles me;
as if shouts are visiting

again; I have fallen down,
the fat colonel looms over

me, he carries the effigy
of the executed in his hands

while the soldiers work on.
This is my dream

in the early morning—,
such a dark, dark time, my love.

Plain-Speaking

After Seamus Heaney

Against the crumpled sheet of white
paper, a glaring carrot, distorted,
it looks like the naked arm of a man,
fingerless, shoulder-less, just the arm
resting on a rumpled bed, bloodless.

"Although spontaneous in appearance
—[his] work is methodically preplanned."

From here you see the inside of a burnt-out
barn, the broken canvas, the useless
wagons, parked here a century ago—
the sand consuming everything.

Novela

This low-bellied cloud cover
over Lincoln surprises me—
the air is muggy, and a strange
foreboding comfort settles.

In the novel I will never write
it is the last day of their meeting
though they do not know it,
but this is the opening scene of the book,
and after this the deaths begin.

The couple arrives in the tree-full courtyard,
a ritual repeated each weekday
for a decade, though for festival season,
and the feast days, they've stayed away.

They wait for the teasing accidents
of the unseen pianist—always an open chord
not in the same key; and then a quick
wayward arpeggio in the higher notes.

Then the full composition, full-bodied,
a nameless air, though they never
speak, so all they offer are smiles.
Who knows what the other knows?

The couple dances—in the novel, they have
danced for ten years, a man and a woman,
nameless, voiceless, just two bodies
seeking assurance in the ritual.

Here in this moment of the book,
the piano is silent. They stare
at the balcony—the curtain flaps
as usual, but no sound, no music.

Then a portly woman with a bandana
carrying a heavy rug, steps out, looks down,
and smiles. She never existed before.
She drapes the rug over the railing.

It is Persian, curlicues of blue and red,
epics unfolding in the soft light.
The couple looks away, embarrassed,
she leaves first, he follows.

The rest is the world collapsing in,
a city regulated by guns,
leaders betraying leaders,
money changing hands,

wars, and rumors of wars,
snowfall in the summer,
a veritable feast for the poets
who have mastered the jeremiads

of doom. It was always this way
for them, the man and the woman,
and the courtyard was their shelter
of deep secrets—the kind that accumulates

over years and years to become
a monument of betrayals,
though nothing happens,
everything happens,

for in a time of calamity
while a nation folds in and starts
to feast on its own innards,
so much blood, so little peace,

every instant of peace, every escape
into music is an act of abandonment,
every poem, a deep sin, every brushstroke,
a betrayal, every silence, a wounding.

On a day as gray as this, the end
of things seems imminent, Lincoln's

skies are wide as the prairie, the naked
eye cannot see the limits of this gloom.

I think of this novel of deep silence,
as a way not to think of those waking
to bury their violently dead,
those heavy searching for a narrative

of anger to allow them to face
the day. When my father died suddenly,
I sought out the villains quickly,
they kept me company for years,

they gave me anger for sorrow,
they gave me the stoic seething a son
of a dead old campaigner should bear,
they gave me reason to replace

the incomprehensible. Tomorrow
I will protest the infestation of guns,
but today, I sit in the shelter
of this city's darkening morning

and contemplate the choices of fiction,
as in who returns the next day,
the man or the woman? I know
one will not. I still can't tell which.

The Scent of the Cankerworm

Someone has promised snow—outside in the half light
I can tell from the heavy sky that the air knows when
the silence will come over us again, and white will
blanket everything. I was not born to snowfall,
still, I have understood the metaphor of shelter
and how a man, walking out into the evening after
a day in shadow, can be filled with something like hope
at the transformation that snow enacts—a painter
abandoning color for the shades of gray and light;
the simplicity of it all, and the grand silence.

Yesterday, a man asked me what are we to do,
for something must be done. I told him to do
the things he has always done, and he said it is
not enough to do what he has always done, and I
said I would do what I have always done, which did
not please him for he wanted to change his ways,
and I thought to say, "See, there is a small pond
by the roadside, what is stopping you from being
dunked into a new holiness?" but what I said
was nothing, I had nothing to say to him because
I dared not imagine what sins he wanted to set
aside, what inaction he may have regretted.
I continue to do what I have always done, knowing
the old equation of our days—I cast my stones
as one who may be stoned, and each day I shed

the burden of regret, stand on the upturned bucket
and say, "I am the least, and so I can say that beneath
the muting of snow, the worms are simply waiting
for the thaw." This is what I do, I keep the scent
of the cankerworm's efforts in my nostrils, it is
what I must do in the epoch of the mute and the deaf.

Dawn

If in the blue gloom of early morning,
the sky heavy with portents of snowfall,
the air crisp with the cold that will
gather about us for the long season ahead,
you see the slick blackness of my car
humming in the empty A lot; and if you
see the light of the dash against
my face, and notice my mouth moving
like a sputtering madman's might,
and if you see me wave a hand
toward my head and pull away
the knit tam I wear close to the skull,
and if you see me rocking, eyes
closed—then do not second guess
yourself—it is true, I have been
transported into the net of naked
trees, above it all, and my soul
is crying out the deep confusion
of gospel—the wet swelling in my chest
is the longing in me, and these tears
are the language of the unspeakable,
"I don't believe he brought me this far, to leave me."

Chadron

There is here, the vague light
of frontier—flat, even land,
no mountain in sight and all
that sky; and the wind is cold
here on the left edge of the state.
Next are the cowboy states—
Wyoming, Montana, Utah and those
myths adored by that half-deaf
tree trimmer, the motor
of the chainsaw has made him
incapable of applause,
as if he will collapse like
a shell-shocked soldier
at the shattering noise. He speaks
in crusty iambics, he wants
to wear boots and stomp into
the blue fields to eat beef
and live the gnarly life
of an old hero. This land
produces linebackers,
they can't catch a ball
due to the wind but know how
to hold onto bodies, tightly,
and crush them. I am
a strange statue in the wind.
My skin darker than the earth.

My gray beard a warning
against familiarity.
We leave in a light drizzle,
the pool cleaner says, "fifty
em-pee-aich winds, bud,
drive careful."

Sandoz Revisited

Layered, she stands against the biting
wet wind; the reservation to her back.
She is not used to the sound
of drums; still, the wind
has carried away from her—
the edge of blood lost
to the sky. She will write
her grand fictions, of tiny,
hard-boiled women, beaten
leathery by the cold discipline
of the patriarch father;
he of seven wives, three dying
in midwinter, two disappearing
in high summer, headed
east, they said, preferring
some Pittsburgh tenement
to the cellar punishments
of this big-headed Swiss
autocrat. The daughter
will outgrow his will,
outgrow his power to hold,
outgrow his capacity for blood;
and so, without fanfare,
with the calculation
of a prospector; she leaves
at the end of harvest,

for the city at the eastern edge
of the state; and from there,
she enacts her vengeance
with stories, blustery as the wind
hurtling over the prairie, loaded
with the echo of chanting,
the stick and leather of drums;
the hint of bloodletting,
the language of a lamenting tribe;
and the old man dies alone
in February, the house
covered in snow; the body
preserved for a spring
burial; in the everlasting
light of a new season.

The Enemy of Memory

For Carolyn Forche

And though we are not most people, we know enough to know that most people
are not most people. It is another motto for this state that has tired of its
   own insecurity
and inferiority, and to preempt the jokes, have enshrined a new motto—Nebraska,
it's not for everyone—which is funny only if you are not an alien arriving for
   the first time
in midsummer, shocked by the long day, the blank inertia of the faces—not
   for everyone,
but for whom? As if this means something. To the poet I said as if I had
   caught her in a lie—
that in your memoir you remember such details; how many rabbits was it,
   and the siren
of flies, and the scents and the gestures of the campesinos, and the quality
   of light,
and every meal, and the ways you seduce me as novelists tend to but they are
   certified liars.
And she said with umbrage, It was just forty years ago and I wrote a daily journal—
I still have a cardboard suitcase full of yellow notepads on which I took
   notes, wrote letters,
drew faces badly, and marked like tiny fences the bodies I saw—the dead ones—
I know now that all countries hide their dead and we have learned to shield
   our eyes
from their shame—like learning a language slowly, this art takes some learning—
the longer I stayed, the less strokes for my fence—an art of deception,
   delusion, survival.

And her words came as a righteous cutting down and I thought that my
        words written down
are the enemies of memory—how I savor the pleasures of my life by being stingy
with my poems, stubbornly denying them the words held in a kind of beauty—
once written I have committed them to a death and I know why she never
        told me this
all these years. It's because none of that happened—no questions asked, for
        the day
I hoped to ask, she was in another state, recovering from age. I am walking
        in rainfall today,
my heart in gross repose dreaming of Accra and that unwritten sweetness I
        hold inside me,
what a memory of childhood shaping—the myths of love the myths of one's
        making,
the taste of yoyi, the platter of kelewele, the sweet peppery burning of light
        soup and fufu;
the lamentations, the hymns, the anthills, the dancers turning, the firm
        mothering hand
of a woman who commands your days; what I cannot speak for the sin of it,
the transgression of it; and I think that I have been born into an epoch of
        terrifying sights,
the things we cannot undo, the way death is held on screens, the blood, the
        grotesquery
of severed limbs. In these walks, leaping over puddles, I do not expect to see
        the carcasses

of war and this is comfort. Instead, I count my meals, a fist of almonds, a
   slice of cheddar,
a frothy latte and all this artificial light of the computer, I feed on yearning
   lines sent to me
in morsels of haiku, I comment simply, glance only, as modesty demands
   when the flash
of underwear peeks and vanishes. This is the language of healing on days of
   lamentation.
I am saying to the poet of witness, we live these days as priests in garments
   of mourning.

The Poor Man's Sacrifice

I have taken to collecting doves, random shades, and feathers, I am not
particular, they do their job. But of late, in the hill country, the doves
have fled—the news has arrived that the sacrifices have turned into slaughter,
and the one with hands stained with his sin is relentless in his
faithfulness and his obsession. I have become the collector of fresh
river water, buckets and buckets, that I leave out in the sunlight,
and without query, I carry out the ablutions on the southern wall, I scrub
away my woes. This is the path of the mourning who returns each day
to the corpse, who soils his hands on the fetid remains, and though it is true
that memory is merely the revenant of flesh, the tears are deep salty and
    they come
in rivers that leave a film of filth—the filth of the mourner on all things.
There is a lie in all sorrow—it pretends nobility, the rituals of regret, but mostly,
my body has taught me that it is greedy for touch, it is greedy for transgression,
it is greedy for the signs that soon, even the most squalid of pleasures
will be gone. I have not grown silent, friend, I have merely sealed all the noise
in my head. On my walks, I carry stretches of verse in my head, then swallow
them quickly like the orgasm sucked in out of sudden disinterest, the
    un-languaged
sorrow—hoping desire will not return. This is the aborted desire of art
and lust or whatever is called the need for that hint of humanity in pleasures
of the body—and the winter is a terribly sweet affront each day—how cold it is,
a flagellating brusque wind that I welcome on my skin, *Oh, whip me, let me feel
that dizzying sensation of aliveness and the deep drunken pain of thawing,
the warming body!* I sleep and dream of the bears in Montana, multiplying
in their numbers, while the ranchers bide their time, await the word to come

that the slaughter of animals is a ritual of healing that the land needs. Here
    is a saying;
the pioneers are slaughtered and the settlers prosper. We heard this too late
for us to decide about Nebraska. Are we settlers? We have no rifles, no wagons,
and this is the way that a new land grows old on you. We have been leaving
since the day we arrived. We do not plan to go west. That too is a settler's
state and the sea beyond is violent as the most resentful reaction of the earth
to the chaos of the settling. Things will return to normal, I am sure, and this is
why these lines, though deeply tempted not to, stop short in the march
    across the page,
still stretch over breaks and hiccups to make for a long breath of hope,
    maybe, or joy.
There is a postscript: the collecting of doves is mere metaphor. I have no stomach
for blood sacrifice, this is the truth. What harm have they done, what value
can I find in the spilling of blood, and why must one be the blood avenger of
    all sin?
The truth is that I commit my sins of the flesh privately and in my own cloister,
no one knows, no one will know, none but the cooing doves who delight in
    my complaints.

Bones

The broken yolk stains my bread. I am waiting here for the fresh snowfall,
to cover the filth of dusty yellow in the city—there is something reassuring
    about
the renewal of things. I know, I know, that held inside each flake is a legend
of our destruction and decay, and still I am waiting for the new fall, as if it is
    still
the first act of delight to hold my mouth open and let the snow fall into my
    throat—
oh alien that I am, I come before these winters with a heart of the rain forest
    dweller,
a man who was raised in a city of thick trees, riotous fruit, and the rot of goat
    shit,
the staining of the walls with their sweat, and the residual of the wheat of
    the ordinary
people: we smell our mortality each day, this funk, this deep consuming
    funk is as heady
as desire. You tell me in a text you paid a boy to shovel the snow. Don't you
    miss me, dear?
I wasn't to ask, but instead, grow silent. In truth, I have been reprimanded
    by my own guilt
for how easily have I silenced the noises of a world entering the terror of a
    dictatorship,
how I have pretended that in time it will pass—how I have carried in me the
    hope in
a constitution that says that in another five years, the terrible order will
    change—

a kind of jubilee and yet I know that I am ignoring the bones scattered in the
    wake
of this horror, the deaths, the losses, the wounds, the debilitating wounds
    that will not heal;
how a generation of infants will have learned that the adults are allowed to
    sulk and scowl
in tantrums and no one is bold enough to do much about it—how the secret
    of the adult
is that we live in compromise each day, we seek our pleasures at the expense
    of others,
and this is enough for us as long as we remain silent. Hope, many have said
    "in these sad
times," and yet in a language that is the language of resigned acceptance? A
    woman hands
me an image of bones; in truth they look nothing like bones at first, but the
    blanched joints
of sugarcane stalks twisted in the formation of improvisation, a kind of neat
    chaos that,
in the blur of half seeing suggests the raising of hands in praise or
    desperation,
the reaching for the thing surging away, their hands watching god and
    reaching for him
and wondering at the elusive terror of ascension, "Savior, Savior, why leave
    us like this?"
But closer up, I see the skeletal composition, something Greek, maybe—that
    ancient ritual

of bones before they have found one another, bones in the instant before
    they start to move,

bones of our lower limbs, the bones she has planted like stalks—yes cane
    stalks,

into the ground—it is called an installation, that is the language for it, and
    no doubt

the artist, her name being Grave, has a macabre wit, though, I imagine that
    when she is

drunk alone at night, it is not ironic, just a deep prophesy placed on her by
    an ancestry

that cares little for what it has left behind. And yet, I know that she has
    given me a gift,

these bones, these dry bones, rising out of the flat surface of the slab of clay,
    polished

as all good museums know they must be, and I know that I can conjure her
    lines of bones,

when I think of the urge to deafen myself to the acts of the tyrant in his
    world of tyranny,

to say that what you are making, a rule, there at the edge of your nation, is a
    graveyard

of bones, dry, broken bones, with no hope of resurrection, and this is what
    you have left.

This is the noise I do not want to fill my head, I do not want to overtake my
    day.

Sponge

From above the snow has turned to a thick patina of gray
the news from the Platte is of snowmelt consuming cornfields
and we on high ground walk in spongy ground crisp with flecks
of ice saying to those calling with concern and alarm,
not here it's dry as chips and winter is reluctant about leaving.
We are camped out in our familiar rituals now, sometimes we slip
into our small boxes, write tantalizing missives to hearts
that are so far away it does not matter, and then we draw near
for stewed sardines, laughter, and the reliable pleasures of films
and cooking shows, everything is intimately distant—so we are numb
to nightmares—how easily in midwinter we hibernate, the tyrant
running rampant through the world, and we, I confess, are used to this.
Close the door, silence the news, or merely ration—no one wants a cyclone
to surprise them. I know that this is a kind of holiness—being set apart,
a monkish cloister, a retreat, but for once I admit that even the saints
knew the secret of a selfish heart, holy onto God, holy onto visions,
holy onto the sacrifice of flesh; the priest after all, never starved,
not, anyway, until the nation was already dead—suffering makes us pray,
and the priest after offering the best fat, gets the second fruit, set aside;
while in the midst of lamentation, the priest is on the hill counting beads.
The violent dead earn two days of mourning, a nation can take little more,
and then we await the new terror, or what we call with scant thought
a tragedy—how they mount, these layered tragedies. Believe me
I am a walking lamentation, I know that my stolid righteousness
my contentment has been eroded by death, I know that Aba's passing
has left me not angry, not broken, not weeping, not anymore anyway

but broken into—as if the backdoor has been yanked from its hinges
and the intruders are slipping in, raiding me of all fortitude.
I have no language for this, something like the loss of ambition for good,
and soon I will find myself walking through a house ravaged by weather,
the walls flimsy, the furniture thin and flakey, and the sound of wind
rushing into hollow places will be my symphony. You do know
that only in language can this be seen, outside there is sunlight
and the world pushes on and the man in a cap and windbreaker
leaning into the wind, is smiling, counting: calories, steps, grams, words;
remarking at the spelling of ukulele and sending condolences
for the old poet dead, and remarking to himself how
the young poet who has chronicled her life on Instagram, Revlon-faithful
devotion to her looks, is older now and seems bloated with birthing
which is its own lyric—the emptiness of ambition.
Flying over this county, the gray Platte spreads over land, consumes
houses, slowly, a canker to the soul, a casual devouring of the land
teaching us the pace of the tragedies of our days, slow, steady, an inundation
of decay—the rot sets in deep beneath the surface of things, the sponge.

On History

A disquiet settles inside my blood,
a slight vertigo before the nausea
that lasts despite the snow-burnished light. God
returns as do most rituals I measure
my joys with. In truth, I find no pleasure
in history, and it is all I consume
these days: the nineteenth century, mass murder,
the Ku Klux Klan, black bodies broken, gloom,
doom, and pernicious injustice for years to come.

The Epoch of Lies

Now is the epoch of grand inventions, and so
the tongues of liars are golden, precious
things. I watch the open hand of the beggar,
it is pink with privilege, though I can
smell the residue of shit on it and see
the stain of clumsy hygiene in the even
nails. I offer to this hand the gift
of my dreams, elaborate tales of the seductions
I have conducted on roadsides;
my body moving off the road into
the sea of aromatic prairie grasses
only to be found out by the brown
bodies of irritable twins—they wear
stained khaki blankets over their shoulders
like monks, so that their nakedness
seems holy, a kind of earth-
dull ordinariness. I did not seduce
anyone—I was seduced by a simple
lie, they promised my fruit
that would harden me for the swampy
journey. The beggar withdraws the hand
complaining of the wetness. Sniff
it, I say, for I know that what will
fill all nostrils will be the clean revelation
of lemongrass. "Bread and coins, I have
not, but herbs, these I give to you,

fill a tub and marinate yourself in
the luxuriant scent of sweetgrasses."
I return to the roadside. The car
is humming in the cold air.
The road is empty. Across the fields,
the sky has started to darken.
It will be hours before I arrive.
You will believe this too;
and do not feel duped by
what I have to say. We are all citizens
of the city of the deaf.
It is our fault, yes, but then again
who knows how to see after learning
the mechanics of lifting eyelids?
That, my dear, is a finer art.

Sea and Rain

Upstairs, now, before eight o'clock,
in the Midwest a cold wind throws

leaves against the pane, and the nights
come down quickly—and it is

before eight o'clock; you left
my meal of rice and lentils on the table.

I am not hungry, you said
in the tender voice of love, though

I know now that it is the tiny
eye at the center of a growing

storm whirling behind the door
of our room. The dog is asleep

early, as if she knows not
to whimper at our door. Upstairs

the room is thickening with
clouds and rain, a heavy grayness

that is mute behind the walls,
and I am waiting for the washing

machine to sing again, waiting
for the wind outside to become

a steady moaning, before I come
up, stretch on my back, and listen

to the first spray of rain, then
the deluge, then the swirling

floating bed; both of us weeping,
two dumb corpses; without language,

without the substance in us
to reach across the divide

and let our fingers touch,
entwine, hold on.

Purple

For Akua

Walking, I drew my hand over the lumpy
bloom of a spray of purple; I stripped away
my fingers, stained purple; put it to my nose,

the minty honey, a perfume so aggressively
pleasant—I gave it to you to smell,
my daughter, and you pulled away as if

I was giving you a palm full of wasps,
deceptions: "Smell the way the air
changes because of purple and green."

This is the promise I make to you:
I will never give you a fist full of wasps,
just the surprise of purple and the scent of rain.

Forgetting

For Jack Doyle

I built a sentence as I would a house of cards;
of course, I learnt how to build a house of cards
years ago—and even though I can't recall
what a house of cards is, I know I built one,
and then for a year, I built one every day
and tore it down. I learned my way
around a house of cards, not like I have
moved around this new city. Here, I have become
a slave to the prodding of a woman's voice
saying "recalculating," like a reprimand,
and I have the feeling of being perpetually
a stranger in this new flattened city where
the natives find their way with cardinal points;
I am forgetting things, too, these days,
like how to get from here to there, or people's
names, and the old alphabet trick of miracles
works no more. So, I pretend that it's
normal even when my chest tightens
with panic for a second, and I remember
laughing Jack when he walked from room to room
to say goodbye, to say that in a few months
he would have gone into another country
where no one will know his jokes—gone
to never return—or the day two years later
when I saw Jack standing alone in the parking

lot, and he was long gone; we had no more language

to share. These visions of Jack last a second,
and then I forget to feel afraid. Marvin, the eighty-
year-old soccer player, when a name slips
from him, turns around with a little jig
twice, and then stops and says, "Still not there!"
And we laugh.

The Quality of Light

Sun days. Chill air. Sun days. Chill air. A body
moves out of the shadows, searching for sun.
Sun days. They arrive with surprise. A body
has been practicing the dialect of sorrow,
and this light, tender as early dusk light
suggests a smile, a healing smile that floods
everything. Sun days. Chill air. Sun days.
I fear the path to words—they are hanging
over me, these twisted sounds seeking something
like answers, although what they do want
is a narrative that welcomes the days that follow.
It is springtime here in Nebraska.
They tell me the cranes are prancing in the Platte
basin, moving with prehistoric elegance,
so old here, even our bodies feel like alien
creatures, the flat prairie consumes everything,
only ancient things make sense here. The rains
will come each day—spot the concrete roads,
and the governor says the prairie will feed
the world, corn, wheat, and cattle, will feed
the world, for the water table is deep and endless,
for the industry of the people, for the flat
silence of these lands. Here optimism
is celebrated in quiet nods—the chemicals
seep deep into the earth, and soon we will know.
Sun days. Chill air. Sun days. Chill air.

In These Times

These days the codes of our time have not settled into common truth—
shared terrors, if you will. It is easy to mock the hand-wringing,
the lament of "these times" as if across this nation the deep
morass that settled in on those who lost, the wounding and shame
of seeing the winners gloat and then stomp about at rallies,
giddy with the rewards of comeuppance shouting, "We are the ones,
we are the true people, we the people, we the people!" is the same
as every destruction of history—the scholars are using massive
sheets of tracing paper covered with the sure lines of history's
last demagogue, to map out our future and present—it is heady
stuff, this way of learning how things may end. Still some of us
know the way the air feels, electric and thick with the promise
of violence, quick, unremitting, with the logic of pragmatism—
a body is in the way, move it—it is not fear that comes over you,
just the sharpened sense that anything can happen.
I cannot claim with certainty that one morning, I will not step out
into my perfectly bronzed Nebraska street, and not sense the calamity
of bloodshed in the air—but today, everything is still as ritual, we are dying
slower deaths, the canker seeping under the bone, and then
the courts will be weapons, and the rich, now quiet in their mansions,
will be assured of the guards at the gate. It is not revolution
they want, it is the heavy bodies of the resigned, the bodies
who blame themselves for their empty lives, for the coins
they must rub together, of those who enjoy vicariously, the pleasures of those
who built things, looming, gleaming things, edifice after edifice
of progress. On Wednesday, before the rain shimmered across

the prairie and painted the high glass walls a mauve so assured
it seemed like a sign, as if the prophet was saying, "Make your art
this color," I stood in the turning light and stared at this stilled
moment: a rancid greened copper chandelier, the rusted chains
dangling down like rotten-black wisteria; a wall the color of a *dundus*,
patchy maps of whiteness, the peeled plaster as if the disease beneath
the first skin is a history of wounds and abuse revealed; and ornate
pillars pressed into the wall, each wrinkle thick with moss and collected
skin; and then finally, in the foreground the two chairs like worn-out friends,
elegant as art on show, two preserved wingbacks, money written
all over their lines and upholstery—almost kissing, waiting, as if soon
a nation will recall its lost beauty. I could not stop looking at these subjects,
mute in shadow and light, and every metaphor fell apart, every metaphor
except the whispered news that we are all waiting, and in our waiting
we carry in us every history that a body can carry, and this moment,
this caught grace may well be our only salvation for these times,
for these perilous, glorious, confusing, annoying, hopeless, vapid times.

Sugar

I keep returning to the hall of high ceilings, twenty feet up with elegant
    geometrical
frescoes forming a crown of opulence above it all—the chandelier is now green
with rust and all the crystal has shattered, but time has turned decay into art—
only the humid air of this island can turn a wall of layered paint into a Turner
sky of storms and prophetic beauty; and there in the corner, the red piano.
The red upright, the red piano with its tiny patch of stripped paint;
the lid up, the keys tuned exquisitely by the blind woman with her cups of coffee
and her cigars, and her mouth heavy with desire, who tells her dreams to
    the air,
all dreams of her pleasures—always in the forest, always at dusk, always bright
as promise. "This wood," she says, "is mahogany, and I grew up smelling
    the ripe
fertility of mahogany, deep in the forests—this is my favorite piano; it is made
from the wood of this island—they lie, they lie, it is not a Steinway, it is better.
It holds the sound of old slaves left in the woods to die—they sing a song so
    elegant
it will make your skin pimple with desire." The red piano, the red piano—
such sweetness in the architecture of wood and steel and ivory.

I have said it many times before in my head, but never out loud, until a poet
said this to me, "It is best when I think least," and this is truth that helps
    no one.
I make it a grand gesture by the lengthy contemplation, the weighing of this
and that—mostly the procrastinating, though that suggests a weight of meaning
the contemplation of what might be and what might not be, when, in truth,

I am living in the blank gaps of feelings that settle over me like weather does
in the late summer of Nebraska—the suggestion of harvest to come, the script
in the air that natives can read, but I, not born to the farm, to the calculus
of acreage, can only guess at. What I say here grows out of a restless exile.

We are all natives to some acre on this earth—where the honey is gentle
on our skins, and the air is familiar as ritual. We, too, I am told, owned
our own acres, homes of ornate splendor, before the old man, Levi, died
blind to the world. Levi's death certificate holds its promises
and curses—that he was past seventy when he went, that his son, Winston,
the solicitor was present, that this witnessing is listed on the official notice
to be filled, that the disease was known to him for twelve years—a kind of
    prophecy,
as if someone came to him one morning on Upper Elleston Road in Kingston,
and told him that this sweetness in his piss will eventually break him down,
and that in a decade, there tender after days of the last Great War, he would die.

And I mark now the date of my absurd conversation with the doctor, a man
of exotic origins but who chuckles and one-lines like a midwestern frat boy,
quick to get drunk, yet hardy enough to be on the combine before dawn,
blooded by fiscal responsibility. He tells me the numbers in my blood,
that I have crossed the line, "At least it is not cancer," he says, and waits to see
my face—I would call it deadpan, but there is a strange spectrum of stoicism
in this state—how the faces of pioneering people will not betray them ever,
faces that I imagine morph into a million masks when the lights are out
and pleasure of anger is rushing like sugar through the blood—this is how

I get through my days in a crowd of Nebraskans; and this is the face I offer him,
no commitment in my eyes, nothing—it takes an emptying of feeling.

I mark this day as the beginning of my leaving. Ah, Levi Severus, teacher—
the things that stay in the blood—you who thought it right to plant yourself
in Africa while Europe devoured itself trench after trench. *Diabetes Miletus*,
the encroachment of dark, more like the narrowing of light, this is how
    you repeat
yourself in the corners of our lives. Kojo, now blind to the world, and him
    just sixty,
oh, my brother, to think we imagined ourselves capable of free will, to
    think that our only
true freedom is in not knowing what came before. There was Richard,
    born a slave,
then Levi, then Neville, then us—a lineage preserved in the bureaucracy of
    empire,
it has made us, given us a language for how we live and die, and so I am counting
the days, the prophet has walked away—it is true that I live the way the apostles
did after the long shadows of the stinking hill, the common murdering of
    thieves
and traitors—determined to defy the promise of their own deaths by the chaos
of effort, preaching, healing, shaking dust from their feet—I am counting
the days before the narrowing of light to a pinpoint and then all I will have
is the mystery of sound—living on memory, living on the last of the light;
is this what it is like, Kojo, Mama, Felix, Levi, is this what it is like to sit in
    silence

and wait for the darkness to grow its fungus of taste and touch, to become
an old friend? My God, I pray again and again, deliver us from hyenas, my God,
deliver us from hyenas, my God, deliver us from hyenas, my God deliver us.

I keep returning to the hall of high ceilings, frescoes crowning above it all—
the shattered chandelier has turned decay into art—the musty sky of storms
and prophetic beauty; and there in the corner of my failing sight, the red piano,
the ghostly blind woman with her cloud of cigar smoke,
"This wood," she says, "is mahogany, and I grew up smelling the ripe
fertility of mahogany, deep in the forests—this is my favorite piano; it is made
from the wood of this island. It holds the sound of blind slaves left in the
    woods to die—
they sing a song so elegant it makes my skin pimple with desire."

"All Teeth and Smile"

". . . an innocent and playful lot / But most disgusting dirty."

T. S. ELIOT

The uses of Negroes abound, and here
I leave aside the obvious trade in flesh
and labor, so much blood and shit,
and speak of more existential uses.

How to mention the thick-lipped
Negro, Bolo, like a conjuror whispers
the name of Eshun, and hands him
over, a talisman; he means something:

the calculation of freedom in the old refrain,
"There but for the grace of God, go I."
A slave is a wonderful foil for the free;
thank God, thank God, thank God, Amen.

This "nigger" cemetery of trash, disuse,
and neglect—at least this is what old Bloom argues,
(not the white Negro of Dublin fair city,
but Steven's apologist in New Haven).

And there is the use of the Negro—
She, old Gwendolyn, is the cook taking up
space on the wall—so persistent they
are—you can smell them long after they are gone.

And they are buried here, metaphors,
similes, symbols, just one word consumes
our morning; this is Whitman's ruddy
shore, he knew them all too intimately.

Then they are no longer there, but
the lovely meditations on our mortality
dangle like decorations over the squalor,
these are the uses of Negro sweat: I too, I too, I too.

One mention is enough—and soon
no one will quote Wallace, the insurance man,
the inconvenient stone in the shoe. Oh, the use
of the Negro is enough to make all things gray-blue.

Sniper

After a year he has aged
alarmingly; gray and bent
with a tall-old-man-slouch.
He stoops to me,
avuncular grin—bandy-
legged. "Tomorrow
I'm back at war;
Reno is my battleground.
My kit: coffee,
a lemon Danish,
and the Everyman's compact
Whitman for the downtime.
Here's the trigger
finger on the keyboard—
press "send": Ka-Boom! You
are dead. A thousand
miles away. Black
smoke, gray, pink, and red."

Long Distance

Alone in the open plaza, the broad Nebraska sky,
morning gray—she sits on a bench, legs crossed,
and the language floating in the air is a kind
of music of nostalgia; her body leans in,
compacting herself as if cold, as if squeezing
herself into something small enough to enter
into the narrow channels that travel to some
foreign place, where the earth is red
and the air smells of burning wood, and the rapid
shouting of crowds eking out their daily
living cut into these whispering.
It is early, almost dark in this city—
and it is not hard to tell that she has come
out into the wide-open space so she may
whisper secrets to the receiving body
far away. This is how lives are changed;
this is how lovers confess their infidelity,
this is how a woman says, *In those days,*
you would make sure the water was warm,
before you let me in. You have changed
so much, so much. She grows silent
as I pass, her eyes damp with traveling,
then she looks away, listening, still listening.

Prairie

They will die, grow inert like unused legs, develop
clots that will atrophy the flabby muscles,
then die, these cities dropped in the middle of nothing;
as if nothing is possible in the plains,
as if the interception of a river is a glorious thing,
as if an island suddenly breaking out from
the earth makes the ocean nothing,
as if the plains people saw nothing stretched
like fabric before them, shimmering in waves
of barely or wheat, this is what the city man
said determined to turn the ordinary
patterns of farm folks into something exotic,
special, strange. Of course, the city was not
plopped down, it grows, stretches over
the open fields, mutates, pulses, breathes,
finds its own music, becomes one
with the consuming earth; what is left
is the plenitude of space, the substance
of land imagining newer and newer beginnings.

Pleasure

At the tail end of pleasure, just
when we know it will be over;
we are left to review its meaning,

meaning we must wonder

at what pleasure may have been,
and we do so by the taste—

the foretaste of absence—
only then will we know what
we have lost—what deserts stretch

before us. The house is empty,
so I have colonized one small
path from kitchen to bedroom

where I exist. Deep into the night
I thought to wake and piss
on all corners of the house

to ward off intruders that I hear
in the creak and groan of the building.
But I live in the twenty-first

century and a house
reeking of piss and vermin
is not earthy, not rustic,

just neglected. One contemplates
these things at the tail end
of pleasures. Americans have been

lying about our churchgoing—
apparently, we are a lapsed
people, self-righteous and liars.

I prayed for my friend's
daughter. I prayed
for the president. I prayed

for this empty house to fill. I prayed
at this frayed edge of pleasure.

The Chronicler of Sorrows

Were I better at this, I would study almanacs,
chart the seasons, visit Ted Kooser on his farm
in midwinter, without invitation, and carry
his two-by-fours and barbwire rolls to the edge
of his land, and ask him the names of the birds
turning in the sky, or the yield of the corn crop,
or the number of people he has buried—farm people,
his people. Were I better at this I would drink coffee
in the quaint cafés in western tiny
towns, talk to those wary of me at first,
by then I would have learned the dialect of cattle,
of waterways, of the market, and we could talk
of Coronation market in Kingston, where their produce
would sell, undercutting the machete-armed farmer
from St. Anne's organic yield, the world turning
into a biblical economy of famine and plenty.
I would be the inside man, the reporter, the one
to trace the secret incantation of chemicals,
how they translate into college fees, new trucks,
mortgages; this would be my labor, my art, even.

I am not a better man. Instead I make up stories
like one who has been promised that his sayings
will become the source of proverbs, and he will be
remembered as the lone man, hooded, walking

across the sea-hardened beach where the tide
has receded so far, it appears a lie that soon
the bay will gleam with folds of the Atlantic;
stories like this one about the woman who one
day, without warning, declares herself tired
of words, and leaves her family for a convent
where everyone stays silent and eats vegetables
and stews, and artisan breads, and puts away
all devices that multiply words—she does this
for three weeks, pretending that she is tired
of speaking, but is really tired of hearing the sound
of her husband asking questions about heart,
and fear, and sorrow. So that when she returns
her depression is deeper, and she longs
for another month of empty silence,
for she learns that it is not so much words
she is escaping, but thought, the need
to make sense of things that have now
become too painful for thought. Of course,
she missed the beep of her phone, the friends
asking her where she is—that she missed.

And given the choice, wouldn't you choose
to be the guardian of the earth, instead of this
quite hapless chronicler of sorrows? There is a joke

here, and a proverb: "A man makes jokes
when he fears the joke is on him"—or something
such; next time I will include a pot. I know,
these days, that comedians are sad—why? Because,
they have the dull sorrow that makes funny
things unfunny, and no one beats a deadpan.

July Fourth

It is the Fourth, and I am marking it with domesticated fear, the things I suffer in
*   nightmares.*
The thing I fear most losing is the thing that has kept us through the shadows and
*   storms.*
And love does not teach us the language we need for the hurts we breed in midsummer.

1

And art is a kind of magic; a hallucination of meaning is another way to
    retrieve it.
A cup of tea: With a teaspoon I scrape the skin off the giant ginger root
until a pale bone whiteness, still heavy with held-juice remains; and this I shave
into thinnest slivers over the board still meaty with the scent of shallots,
and these I scrape to one side, holding them in waiting while I roll the
    plump lemons
we bought by the dozen at the Vietnamese market where a small woman in black
shin-length slacks spent ten minutes testing the substance and rightness of
    carrots—
she was looking for three only but dug through a box rolling them in her hand,
weighing them, testing their color and I stood certain that there were
    secrets I did not know,
things that must be hidden from me even as she walked away, staring at the
    three,
then stuttered in her walk, paused, and returned to the box, rummaged
    until she found one
she had abandoned, and she exchanged it for another she had chosen, and
    then she walked

with certainty to the front. I gathered, without ceremony my lemons, which
     I now roll as if

this too is an art, softening the body for the juice to want to spurt forth—I
     slice the belly

of the fruit, place one half on the side board for later, and the other I
     squeeze quickly

into my bowl. Ginger and lime and then the placing of the moringa leaves in
     soft bags—one

with mint, the other smelling like old leaves sun blanched, barely giving
     much back to us

before the slow pour of water, boiled and re-boiled, over the aromatic nest
     and the scent

that rises up smells of an orange grove by an ancient graveyard where even
     the newest

tombs have been broken open and the dead hum their decay in the air,
     where the rotting

oranges are a perfume, a relief for those who handle the dead—we must
     know the scent of

death; this is the magic and the healing in the herb, a kind of poison that
     heals, as old as

all bitter leaves. Something must die for something else to live, I have made
     an art of my tea

making, a ritual for dusks, just when the sun grows bored and the light
     tenders my skin—

I offer her a sip and she receives it with questions in her eyes but trusts the

precision

of the making, she has seen it before, day after day, this is what it takes to
     bring healing.
The thing I fear most losing is the thing that has kept us through the
     shadows and storms.

2

And art is a kind of magic—more the hallucination of meaning: a perfectly
     curved staircase
built of elegant concrete work—the kind old communists would perfect in
     the lazy months
of the Cold War, you know, those months of waiting for the next act, or the
     pointless spying
behind the lines—we lived with secrets as if these were normal, could spot
     an agent
by their slippery walk; and great art is made in those slower times, death
     held at bay
and God hidden behind the plywood separator—the carpenters quietly
     leaving the host
and all the magic of miracles where they were, the white embroidered
     cloths, the chalices,
the robes, the Bible—held there as if waiting for a time for them to be
     recovered intact
as all faith hidden behind history can return intact. And art is the lime
     green of the walls,
the terra-cotta glow of the tiles, the ornate steel-framed chairs, the massive
     dome

on the ceiling, opaque to spread the soft light over everything. Yes, first
    there is a woman
at the top of the stairs, painted with the heavy skin of a black saint—you can tell
that her language is a deep African Spanish, and her head scarf is loose
    enough to release
the thick plaits of hair—her body is that of a mother, a full woman standing there
and watching the slow tortured descent of her children. This splendid
    picture of terror—
the separation, the cry from those leading the children down the
    stairs—expressionless,
this cry, a kind of blow asking, *Why bring them here if you know that they will
    be taken*
from you, what makes you a mother? The magic happens then, a cliché of
    sorts. The children
fade and then disappear, erased, a firm wet thumb wiping the pigment,
    leaving the lime
green walls, then the woman looks up as if to note the dark shadowing of the
    top of the stair,
and this is all there is, a kind of magic. I confess that I have willed my mind
    to not imagine
the happenings at the border, willed my body to push back against the urge
    to supplant
the stoic news reporter with her midwestern accent, to push against the
    urge to itch,
then shudder with a memory of my mother, holding her face, a soldier's

palm embossed

on it, and a minute ago he was "my son," and then he was the brute doing his job
to keep the line moving, and we were on holiday in Accra just a minute
    before and suddenly
we became refugees, hoping to flee, and our cousin the field marshal, would
    step in
with the cold calm of an executioner, and in my heart, at least, I wanted as
    much to plead
for that man as I did to hear him plead before the revolver shot in his head.
That is the nature of terror, and its language, that is the magic, to make it all
    vanish,
to make my mornings bland, a suburb at seven-thirty, quiet as that long
    hiatus of peace,
and all my mind dwells on are the deprivations, the body's desire for
    affection denied,
the fear of a lover's disdain. I live here in this moment, standing at the top
    of the stairs,
and all art can be magicked into romance, and this is all we long for in the
    most perilous
times. Do not intrude on my interim of sanctity, do not quote the veteran
    who chuckles
that we are a brutish species, that we arrived at the top because we are
    brutish, blood-
hungry machines, and war, he says, is not the place to teach us the art of
    suspended
empathy; no, war is the finishing school of our deepest selves, and this,
    softly grim prophecy

is the noise I do not need today on this Fourth, neighbors lighting
   gunpowder, relishing
the explosions, these ceremonies of revolution, the dog whimpering under
   the table.

It is the Fourth, and I am marking it with domesticated fear, the things I suffer in
   nightmares.
The thing I fear most losing is the thing that has kept us through the shadows and
   storms.
And love does not teach us the language we need for the hurts we breed in midsummer.

III

On Blindness

These may be the edges of a long gloom—
Dr. Pfeil, o d , gangly harbinger of shadows

promises new ways of seeing, the comfort
of modern technology, but he too knows

the shadows will begin at the edges.
The cells, the ganglia cells, are dying,

everything is dying—I write the litany
of my inheritance: a grandfather in 1940

falling into gloom before the valley
of the shadow; another in 1975, he too calling

for a bowl of water to rinse his fingers before,
before, before feeling for the lips and eyes

of the grandchild, amazed at the intimacy
of sightlessness, these substances of the dark

we imagine; and now you, Mama, in your closing
shadows, waiting for a sound for silence,

how deep inside your blood you live,
these days. I crowd my days with the depression

of novelists, those who have forgotten
how to laugh, and the day turns to night.

Clocked out so long ago, as if the color red
has lost its anger. This is September.

The emptiness stretches toward the Nebraska
horizon, a shifting oppression of sky.

Insomniac

Below the surface the marble aqua
of the mosaic gives comfort;
as if the suggestion of light
deep in the stone promises distance,
whole vistas—I have learned
that the swaddling of mountains
extends my sleep—the mist
in the hills, the finite space
of a valley, the cave
of a comforter heavy
as the green and gloom
of those mountains—I sleep
deeply because I am
rehearsing death; but here
in this wide sky of prairie lands
I have discovered the priceless
friendship of the insomniac,
that man in dungaree
overalls with his shovel
and horsehair paintbrushes,
wincing into the open sky,
his patient hand drawing
streaks of blue over a blank
surface—he talks and talks
in tidy stanzas, every breath
a new efficient epic—I doze

off for a minute and wake
to find his voice rattling
away—leaves, fences, long
rides, the trunks, dogs, the wind-
storms, storms, and trees.

Bed Time

I wake to hear Ted Hughes with his
posh accent scream expletives
at Sylvia, sending her weeping
into what I imagine to be a cold
Yorkshire grayness—though I have
been there, and green was
the oppression, a kind of chaotic
crushing vegetation. Then she returns,
her voice timid as smoke,
saying, "Please don't leave me."
My wife's breathing is not deep,
which tells me she is alive
and in half dream half alertness
in her heart to the tragedies
of the day; and I imagine
as I drift away, the logistics
of filming a woman head first
in an oven; and Sylvia's sadness
covers this dry Nebraska night,
where everything is muted
by the unending despair of snow,
wishing I had warned her against
the callow haunting of the film.
Still, I fall asleep, while the voices
grow muffled, and I hope
deep in my skin, for her hand
to rest on my lower back,
warm, confident as lasting love.

Transplant

Transplanted again the storehouse
of words for things is a waste.
It would be like Adam after
the garden; he had no notebooks,
no satchel of ledgers, just the memory
of names; all of which flew out of his head
when the woman came; she only
had to hear them once,
and she gave them all nicknames,
she stood while they danced
around her—it was like that;
and when they stepped
out of the old plays, even
the familiar things lost
their names; too busy
as they were chopping wood,
counting out the days,
calculating the economics
of light, rain, and moons,
and he could barely
remember the names for God;
beyond the flesh, bread,
and root, he had no taste
for nuance; no pleasure
in the divides of sweetness—
I am saying that here, even

without the flaming sword
barring access to memory.
It is all gone from my head,
what is left is the fuzz
of broken memories, and anyway,
nothing translates to the lingo
of new bones, new light.
It grows dark quickly here,
and God no longer strolls
the gardens, calling out
the name of things with delight;
not even the damp clump
of a name. These days, I must
learn the names of grasses,
shrubs, and the stunted flowers.

Surviving, Again

I am growing fat
and soft in these mid-
American cities, thankful
for the prophylactic
of a wide lawn and a fence.

My neighbors keep their distance.

Some cities will harden us,
and bloodletting farm towns
make us callous, leave us
to negotiate nerve pain
and hypertension.

Numb, now, I relish suburban dullness.

I have heard of your loss,
the wounding you keep
buried in you, and all along
I know I have blocked it out,
securing the borders of this *pest-house*.

I tell people I am preserving myself.

I know too well
the taking down of men like me

by the stress of seeing,
the things that turn our blood to stone,
and calcify our hearts.

I am fleeing from the dead.

These days I walk away
from all the things that remind me
of what I cannot flee.
I argue less, and I let the fools
continue their fool-fool ways.

I am not proud of it but at least I am alive.

Sancho Panza

My sisters told me they thought the servant
clown—"squire" I think was the translation—
but I can't remember why. That was thirty
years ago, perhaps more. But they would
rehearse the complaints he made at being
beaten, and the way he stripped the delusional
knight of his dignity while still keeping
a shred of grace in all that he did. This was
a strange kind of beauty, they spoke it
with laughter. Now I understand the genius
of Cervantes, and the comfort I find
in the sinful ways of Sancho Panza, how entirely
holy he seems in his flawed indulgence,
in his self-serving heroism, in the pure
comic power of his gentle cajoling of the Don,
illustrious fool. I am walking with them
these days, navigating my neighborhood
of fall dryness, every other house with its roof
colonized by roofers laying tiles,
as if there has been a boon on cut-rate
supplies, but it was just this one hailstorm,
and the roofers are making a killing. It is,
though, the story of Cardenio and Lucinda
that litter each mile mark of this walk,
each house, each spot, a kind of dying
of my world in the mood of lament, regret,

violence, and lurid melodrama, and so
this flat, bland city Lincoln has assumed
the shape and texture of stony foothills
where a heartbroken man tortures
himself by not killing himself, his mind
rehearsing the betrayal of love—all quite
lurid. It is how I push back against
the noise of blood and the looming
prospect of a diabolic comic sneering
his path into power. These are brief
sabbaticals, as satisfying as a mindless
soap, but somehow full of the edification
of brilliant language—the stuff that outlasts
the reign of kings, tyrants, emperors,
the rise and fall of empires, hegemonies,
and monstrosities. Each day, as the air
cools, and the world turns into an orange
wash, light softening as it always does,
there is a brief respite, and then I return
to time, its ordinary enslavement,
the body's decay, the counting of coins,
the annoyances, the laughter, the art
of making poems, and this, too, is good;
the kind of thing a good squire must embrace,
bruised, bewildered, and still able to stand.

The Messiness of Place

". . . place is messy"
KEI MILLER

Briefly, as they say, in Leeds, the sky left me
bewildered, like an alien trying to decipher
the noises in the air. There is a heaviness
that comes with being a stranger until one
surrenders to the dialect of tones—as if reading
the language of birds and wind, and the sky.

The sky in Leeds crowds in, consumes space,
carries the quality of tumult and constant action,
as if portending doom—all of this, I admit,
is in contrast to the flat postapocalyptic glare
of the Nebraska sky—this is how it seemed
before all things, and after the cataclysm.

Either way, the sky teaches us how to prophecy
the end of the world. My native tongue is the epic
unscrolling above the Blue Mountains, so that we
in the foothills, on the plains of Mona, would constantly
look to the hills to read our fate. I once lay stretched
out on a Saturday, on a clay-caked cricket pitch,

and I read the sky, the chase and swirl, the deep
hues and light filigree of wispy clouds, and soon
I could predict the arrival of storm—this gave me
comfort, a kind of peace, for I knew in nineteen seventy-
seven, that a powder house would explode; I knew
well, Paul's calm celibacy of devotion, *For this world*

in its present form is passing away, and under
the deluge, I prayed in sobbing thanksgiving, for, as if
a magic had happened here, I could tell the storm
would arrive, even when the sky seemed disinterested,
and this knowing, this sense of sure doom was a comfort.
For the first time I believed I had arrived in a native place.

Ambulation

At the corner of a number and a flower
I think of permutations for a jackpot,
and I think I see the way a moon
can turn you giddy with relief—
the muttering of leaves over brittle
grass is another kind of comfort—
what it is not—not footsteps, not
the first dig before the spring to leap
of a feral dog. Of course, there are
no feral dogs here, behind the soft
light in windows are shelves full
of guns and my neighbors drive
out into the cornfields to release
their temper—they are still angry
with the president for being so
different and tricking them, they
are too decent to say—instead
they release bullets at the moon,
the same moon; it goes without
saying, that I meet at the corner
of a number and a bland popular
flower. I count the pace of an old speech
I learnt by heart thirty-five years ago—
over and over in my head,
"She should have died,"
I say, "The queen my Lord is dead"—

a hymn for the depressed and the once-fat
now disposed creature
walking along the battlements,
that moon washing the woods,
shifting in the shadows; I count,
I walk, ambling, ambling.
This is the last of the fall days,
the trees are bare; the light is clean.

Falling Away

1

There are days that shift from a kind of morendo, all things falling away,
and much of that is redundant, like a young boy staring at an old man
and saying, "You will die before me, bitch." And this is a way to laugh,
for the boy imagines himself with a dagger, a kind of insult. This morning
as if in a dream they said bombs, Somalia, and there was the usual count—
and it has been months since I have heard those words, and I have let my dreams
filter out the narrative of people who are living like this each day, as if there
    is nothing
but the sound of bombs and Somalia—there are other words. The body in
    this state
of morendo is being guided in its sorrows and mourning by the filter of a
    feed—
who is feeding us, what are they feeding us? Such a diet of controlled attention.
I am feeding on a diet of silence, a diet of deafness; this is the way music
    dies away.
I have avoided words in music for weeks now, as if I do not want to be seduced
by the art of words, and so I am composing images against the rise and fall
of instruments—this is my new diet of boiled eggs, English cheddar, and
    pistachios.
I admit that when I void, I feel as if I am ready for new sorrows; this is what
    falling away
is like; this is what falling away is like. There is a rabbit hole of beauty when
    we follow
the voice of Aretha Franklin to her birth—that journey backward, and I stop
    at the church,
and I cry there, for this is my hope the language of the healing art. I have

no doctrine to satisfy the needy, just the rise of her voice over me, and this
    is my new diet,
the morendo, Aretha, you know how you do it, how you abuse us, drag us through
the shattering light of your sound, and then, as if to say, "Roll over now and
    sleep—
and pass me the water," your voice is human again, and in that softness is
    the most tender
and broken thing in the world, which is the secret of all art, the falling away.

2

Between the lumpy porridge of my sick on the light oak floorboards, there is
    a grand
swoon, Lorna nudging me, telling me, Okay, okay, with that comforting
    humor in her
urgency—somewhere I know she is calling, and then with the faint sound of
    alarm,
they arrive—how long has it been? There is no poetry here, just the blur of
    the startling
light, the bright white of the sheet covering my legs, my feet, gnarled and
    sculpted
sticking out, twitching—not dead, not dead; the neighbors I complain, guilty
    that I have
fantasized this moment and a moment of rest; a longing in the fractious
    days in South
Carolina, heavy weighed with my sins, and betrayals and the enemies
    arrayed on the hill,

the hands asking for this and that—in an old poem I said I long for that moment
when I can be wheeled out into a red truck and everyone will go silent; but
    today, everyone
is calm, and I am not dying, but old enough for them to take no chances,
and I do sleep, I sleep so deeply waking only at intersections, like a
    kidnapped rebel
trying to chart where they are taking me—down 70th, down, down, down,
to St. Elizabeth, the hospital where the nurses change shifts as I arrive and
    everyone is giddy
as a social club—welcome, let's make jokes: These guys, these guys are such
    bad luck,
everyone they bring is sick; and I am sure no one has told them it is not
    funny,
but that is humor for you. I doze off again and dream of climbing the art deco
curving stairs made of hand-molded cement and painted with streaks of
    aquamarine
and that bone-sheen white—the paintings on the plaster walls' long frames
    are of the dry arrangement of tropical pods—this is what I dream, my
    body slowly climbing toward
the light coming from the wrought iron window, my face gliding through
    shade and sun,
the shadowed lines, and on my feet the pattern of bubbles spreading like a
    rash of multiplying
cells—the bannisters so carefully chosen. This is not my home, it is a kind of
    retreat,
and in this soft room, Lorna sits to my side, I do not know when she came,

and then I am sleeping, and this is when they say, Nothing wrong, all vitals
    perfect, sometimes
we don't know, sometimes we never know. And I think the secret fear—
    Neville died at fifty-six
after a fall—and I know my children are being brave, though in the morning,
    on a day
defiantly ordinary, they call, "Quite a scare, Pops, quite a scare." I will call
    this house,
morendo; I will call these stairs, morendo—and I take the morning to be a
    notice: Finish
it all, finish the music, finish the unfinished, which is futile really as the
    unfinished
is unknown. And that is the way neighbors smile at me as I stroll the dog
    this morning,
the world humming with mowers, the light smashing the green of the lawns
and the shrubs, and all retarding, all extreme fading, is a kindly myth.

On Picking Battles

Today I wear black jeans, baggy and uncertain—as if waiting for my body
to decide its mind, will you return to the girth or stay here? The loose
fabric confused in its faithfulness. And the priestly black shirt—I wear
black in homage to you, John—the constancy of faithfulness, the simplicity
of a man in his habitual garb of mourning, you are always at war—
I admire this in you. The priests who gutted the sacrifices, the butchery
of holiness, has learned to wear black and carry fresh mint branches
so the scent that carries is not the scent of death—this is the sacrifice
of the warrior. It is how I think of my art, though they say all acts
are art, I have no skin in that game, my haunting is the failure of language.
I do not make for making but for the failure to make my nightmares
in words. And what I see is enough to consume me for how I see
is incomplete. My wife finds comfort in the gloomy shadows, and we
have learned to grin sardonically, the slight irritants of love—give me
constant light, destroy the earth for my light, for I am haunted
by the blurs that I see, the errors of not seeing precisely, a kind
of failure to love what is remembered, and memory comes back to us
as music comes back to us. Forty years ago, we schoolboys whispered that a tree
behind the chemistry lab was special, the character of it was spoken
with giggles and smirks. What you smell? They asked. What you smell?
And the innocents looked perplexed, and the knowing rolled with mockery
and laughter. Only boys can find such deep pleasure in a tree
that smells like a woman's secretion, and now, forty years on,
we ask, does the tree have a name? Is it still there? Will we find it
were we to return, might we smell it? That single tree, sitting in the shadows
of the thick-walled lab—one hundred and fifty years of wood floors soaked

through with the sweat of teenaged boys. I think of a sycamore tree,
or a solitary olive tree, or a burning bush—the joke is ugly as youth—
guileless. These days we are counting the dead, and it is as if we dare
only now, to look—and the number is alarming at first, and then, as with
all losses, each death is a moment of logic or impossible fate, which is
its own kind of comfort—we too will die; we who were not the beautiful ones.
We never ask the question, but it is the one we mean to ask, have you
in all these years, thought of me, or have you forgotten me as I have
forgotten you? And what does this mean about time? What does it say
about friendship. Now I ask about children, about spouses. And some stay silent,
the ones who will not admit the resentments they've carried, the slights
that still sit like wounds on our bodies, we reminisce with a kind of horrific
relish—the cult of belonging. I tell them to read my poems. At least there,
memory is trumped by the truth of feeling, and this is what it must be.
I fear I seem as false as I always was—there is a lie in all sincere acts.
Holiness or truth is as idiosyncratic as the whorls on our thumbs—this is not
orthodoxy, just the kind of truth of faith we learn with age—that one carries
guilt with the expectation of pity and the other sheds guilt as impractical
and in times of war and cataclysm and love such quirks are massive;
they shape our horrors, though, like the tree, like the color of its leaves,
like the pattern of seasons even in the humid constancy of Kingston,
the scent arrives with the worms, perhaps, or the insects, or the dusk,
or when flowers start to suggest themselves, to know the language
of leaves is to know the language of mercy and humility, and I want
to say that the tree's leaves were yellow, and it stood in a muddy strip of earth,
that it shed leaves sometimes, that a plump boy would sit beneath its shade   95

and breathe the scent of woman—his sin, his impractical guilt carried
like a secret. Forty years on, we know now that how we live is made
long before we knew we were learning, that I face the world like I faced
the cricket ball—always willing to bat at number one and face the attack, happy
to get it over with, taking on the heat as a way to soften disappointment.
And a violent act would only happen under the threat of death; the rising
ball, again, after the first one thumped my chest, and so the next one
I fiercely smashed over square leg—the cheering—but me breathing
as one who had barely survived death. Every stroke began with a soft
backward step, always ready to defend, and only provocation moved
me forward, the on-drive, gentle as a reluctant punch, bloodless runs.
I never understood the psychology of the cover drive—such bold anger,
taking the war to the enemy—I made my runs as one forced to act,
and this is a metaphor of how I fight my wars—prepared, willing to draw
blood, and yet, willing to die the death of a martyr—hoping for the lamentation
of those who dare not blame me. On my watch, I fear, the forests will be destroyed.
I must learn the holiness of those whose nights are never haunted with regret,
perhaps the rituals of our garments offer us the heart of deep mourning.
Here come the long-voiced poets, in their flapping black garments;
each day enacting the things we have lost, another kind of holiness.

The Exile Remembers His Sisters

These dark days of being inside and outside—the weather is changing, shifting
to that unpredictable fickleness before the stubborn winter—I gauge my health
in unhealthy ways—this gloom over me, but ah, here comes the wounded, the one
whose sorrow is epic and righteous—suddenly my lament is churlish.
Perhaps this will become my symbol—two chairs, domestic in their placement
side by side, so two sisters may see each other's eyes, but able, still, to stretch
their un-stockinged legs far out over the well-kept rug—the Persian
that would have cost a fortune had it not been picked up at an impromptu sale
of the detritus of the revolution—what the relative who finally got the visa
    left behind
in their haste—not for fear of authorities or the ghostly torturers, nothing so
    dramatic—
just the fear of nostalgia, its haunting hold. They all chose not to sleep
for three days and three nights, for fear that their dreams would shackle them
to the building, to the plastered walls—layers and layers of generations,
    hands upon hands
having restored year after year the smooth surface—to the trees in the courtyard,
their poisonous fruit seeping juice that tie them to their root, to their dreams.
So they did not sleep and left the place as if going off on vacation for a week.
This before the grand sale. And there, spaced evenly in front of the tall
    French doors
with their elegantly crafted wood slates, the star of David set above the jamb
    in a circle
of plain glass against the frame, the doors flanked by two portraits, one of a
    laborer

made with muddy gobs of paint; a Van Gogh composed in the midst of a
    tropical storm—
they left it too, like they left the grave of the grandmother. And to the left,
    the three children,
faces mounted on top of each other, looking out into the room, smiling in
    the way
of inquisitive delight, as if to say, hurry, hurry, take it so I can take mine of you.
If asked, they would say that they left that piece by accident, that they left
    everything
by accident, they left things because the place was dark when they departed,
and such ordinary parts of their lives, the things they accepted as comforts,
    like the scent
of the tamarind fruit rotting in the front yard, or the heavy soapy scent of
    the moss-thick
gutters running beside the kitchen, tucked into a bivouac of a shelter,
    concrete floor
and zinc roofed, coal and logwood, and piles of brown paper, kindling and
    more kindling,
and the black-bellied pots—those things they had to leave behind, for how
    can one carry such ordinary betrayers of culture to the Promised Land?
    Yes, for me the chairs
in the middle of the room, the cushions with golden tassels, the black
    frames, the quiet
elegance of their staging, this is what it means to abandon memory, to
    abandon the myth

of home, and to instead will the abandoned world to people the stage with
　　characters—long
dialogues between sisters sitting face to face, sometimes looking askance,
　　and talking
scandal, loss, desire, fear, the secrets of a nation, the lies of their bodies,
　　the regrets,
a spreading mesh of language clouding the space between their heads and
　　the high ceilings,
their faces refracting the shifting colors of the light falling upon them
　　through the windows,
the epic of time changing from deep purple dawn to the inky silence of
　　night, their voices
going on and on.

Before Winter

I imagine there is a place of deep rest—not in the resting but after
when the body has forgotten the weight of fatigue or of its many

betrayals—how unfair that once, I thought it clever to blame my body
for the wounds in me, the ankle bulbous and aching, the heaviness

in the thigh, and the fat, the encroachment of flesh—it is hard to believe
that there are those who do not know that it is possible to let things

go, to then see the expansion of flesh—it is so easy, and that knowing
is a pathology. What is unknown to be is the clear day of rest—

I carry a brain of crushed paper, everything unfolds as if by magic,
every spot of understanding is a miracle, I cannot take any credit

for the revelations, they come and go as easily as the wind.
You must know that this is a preamble to an epiphany I will record—

the late morning light of October, the damp soiled backyard,
the verdant green lawn, the bright elegance of leaves strewn

over it all, turning nonchalantly in the wind, and the Nebraska sky
blue as a kind of watery ease, a comfort, it is all I can say, the kind

one knows, even standing they're waiting for the dog to squat,
that I will remember for years but will never have the language

to speak of—one of those precious insignificances that we collect
and horde. The moment lasts ten breaths, and in that silence,

I imagine that I can see spirits, I can know myself, and I will not fear
the betrayals of body and love and earth, and the machinations

of emperors and pontificates. It will be winter soon. I know my body
is collecting water in its nether regions, the weight of the hibernating

mammal, storing everything in drowsy, slow-moving preservation,
I mean I am losing myself to the shelter we build to beat back

sorrow and the weight of our fears. I have covered thousands of miles
in a few days, and I feel my parts flaking off, a shedding of yellow

pieces covering the turning earth, and I am helpless to this soft
disappearing, some call it sleep, I will stretch out and breathe.